W9-CCP-413

ADOLF HITLER

CATHERINE ELLIS
AND JEREMY ROBERTS

ROSEN
PUBLISHING®

Published in 2016 by The Rosen Publishing Group, Inc.
29 East 21st Street, New York, NY 10010

Library of Congress Cataloging-in-Publication Data

Ellis, Catherine.
  Adolf Hitler / Catherine Ellis and Jeremy Roberts. — First edition.
    pages cm. — (The Holocaust)
  Includes index.
  ISBN 978-1-4994-6248-7 (library bound)
  1. Hitler, Adolf, 1889–1945—Juvenile literature. 2. Dictators—Germany—Biography—Juvenile literature. 3. Germany—Politics and government—1933–1945—Juvenile literature. 4. Holocaust, Jewish (1939–
1945)—Juvenile literature. I. Roberts, Jeremy, 1956– II. Title.
  DD247.H5E45 2015
  943.086092—dc23
  [B]
                                                      2015018800

Manufactured in China

CONTENTS

INTRODUCTION

Today, Adolf Hitler's name is synonymous with evil. One of the most offensive ways to insult a person is to compare that person to Hitler. Whether or not you would choose to go back in time and kill Hitler when he was a child has become a classic scenario that people debate when they discuss moral dilemmas. Dressing up like Hitler, or wearing the swastika that his Nazi Party adopted as their symbol, is considered deeply shocking and repulsive, even in the present day, when Hitler has been dead for decades.

While Hitler's militaristic, nationalistic leadership of Germany during World War II would be enough to make him unpopular today, the real reason he is so despised is for his role in the Holocaust. The Holocaust—which is also known as the Shoah—was the German government's systematic campaign to wipe out the Jewish people, resulting in the death of about 6 million Jews. Two out of every three European Jews was killed in the Holocaust. Along with Jews, the German government also killed hundreds of thousands of Roma (often known as Gypsies), political opponents to the Nazi regime, gay people, and disabled people.

While anti-Semitism—the hatred of people who are Jewish—certainly did not start with Hitler and the Nazis, nothing else in history really compares

Hitler is not only one of the most despised people in history but also one of the most recognizable. He is especially known for his small, dark mustache. In fact, people regularly refer to mustaches that look like his did as "Hitler mustaches."

to the Nazis' attempts to extinguish the Jewish people as a whole. Attempts to describe and understand the Nazis' actions led to the coining of the word "genocide," which means committing violent crimes with the intention of destroying a particular people as a group. While historians and humanitarians have unfortunately been able to identify other genocides in world history, the Holocaust still stands out, both for how success-ful it was and for how chillingly organized and methodical the Nazis' approach to murdering millions of people was.

Hitler wasn't single-handedly responsible for the Holocaust. All of the top Nazi leaders were directly involved, along with thousands of Ger-man citizens. Some people from countries that the Germans had occupied collaborated with the Nazi genocide, too. While the general public did not know all of the details about the mass killings, the Nazis had led a campaign of persecu-tion against the Jews since they came to power in 1933 and there had been little public outcry against the mistreatment of the Jewish people.

Had it not been for Hitler's own, often-expressed anti-Semitism, though, it is by no means clear that the Holocaust would have taken place. Hitler was rabidly anti-Semitic, blaming the Jewish people for a whole host of Germany's past and current problems. His rousing speeches were a major factor in the rise of the Nazi Party in

Germany during the 1930s, and these were also deeply anti-Semitic. Anti-Semitism was central to Hitler's whole worldview.

Hitler may not have been a good person, but that does not mean that it is not worth learning more about him. It is better to try to understand someone who did great evil in the world than to just pretend that that person never existed. After all, we can always learn from the past and hope not to repeat its mistakes.

CHAPTER ONE

HITLER'S EARLY YEARS

A dolf Hitler was born on April 20, 1889, in the small Austrian town of Braunau am Inn, which was on the border with Germany. His parents were Alois Hitler, a customs official, and Klara Pölzl Hitler, who came from a peasant family. Young Adolf was close to his mother but often came into conflict with his strict father.

HITLER'S YOUTH

As a young man, Hitler wanted to be an artist. He moved to Vienna to pursue this dream after his father's death. He applied to the Vienna Academy of Fine Arts but was rejected twice. He sold small paintings and postcards, but struggled to support himself. At one point, he was so poor he had to beg at a homeless shelter. Hitler disliked life in the diverse, cosmopolitan Austrian capital. After receiving a small inheritance, he moved to Munich, Germany, in 1913.

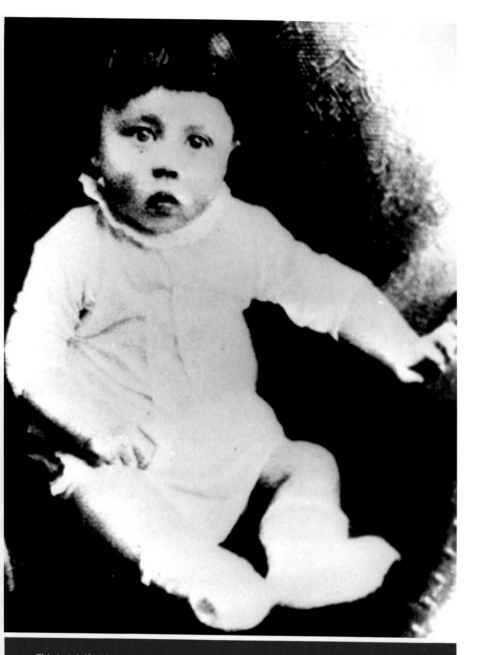

This is Adolf Hitler as a young child. Adolf Hitler had a full sister named Paula, a half-sister named Angela, and a half-brother named Alois.

Like many Austrians who lived near the German border, Hitler's family had German roots. Like many, Hitler thought of himself as German. When war broke out in Europe in 1914, he joined the German army. He won two medals for bravery. He was promoted to corporal. However, Hitler did not seem destined for greatness in the army. No one thought of him as a great leader.

HITLER'S BIRTHPLACE

The house where Hitler was born still stands today in the town of Braunau am Inn. There continues to be controversy over what to do with the building. In 1972, the Austrian government signed a deal with the owner of the building to keep neo-Nazis—people who belong to fascist groups and hate groups that still revere Nazi ideology today—from turning it into a shrine or memorial to Hitler. According to the deal, the building can only be used for government offices, social services, or educational purposes. Until 2011 it was a center for people with disabilities, providing a place for a group of people who would have been mistreated by the Nazis.

Some people have suggested using the building in a way that runs counter to Neo-Nazi views, such as making it a museum about Austria's liberation from the Nazis or a refugee center. While there are people who argue it should be torn down entirely, others say it should stay as a reminder, confronting the Austrian people with the horrors of the past.

WORLD WAR I

Germany did well when the war began. The country surprised France with a massive invasion in 1914. But by the summer of 1918, France and Britain began to win important victories. Behind the lines, Germany had been drained by years of war and a blockade that prevented it from receiving supplies. There was a severe lack of food and other necessary items.

The Kaiser and his government soon realized that surrender was the only way to prevent foreign troops from swarming through Germany. Giving up seemed the best way to prevent more suffering.

This photograph shows the negotiation of the Treaty of Versailles. The treaty marked the official end of World War I and required the Germans to make large reparation payments.

More importantly, it would prevent a disastrous revolution like the one that had occurred in Russia the year before, bringing the communists to power.

Many Germans, however, didn't realize how near defeat their country was. German armies were still on foreign soil. Momentum had shifted back and forth many times during the past four years. Some soldiers felt they were winning. Others felt that they could win, if they just kept fighting. The surrender struck them as a betrayal.

The new government that took over Germany negotiated a peace agreement. Hitler thought the men who formed the government were all criminals. He and others called the surrender a "stab in the back." Their anger remained with them long after the war ended.

CHAOS IN MUNICH

Until he joined the army, Hitler's future seemed dim. In some respects, the army was the best home he had ever known. So Hitler stayed in the army even after the war. He won a transfer to Munich, where he had lived before.

Munich was part of the German state of Bavaria. Immediately after World War I, different factions vied for control. There were riots and uprisings. At the same time, there were many hardships. Food, coal, and other necessities were in short supply. Political turmoil soon led to a revolution headed by local communist groups. In April, these forces took over the Bavarian government. They formed a Red army. Chaos and anarchy reined. By May, these revolutionaries had been defeated with the help of the central government, the army, and volunteer Freikorps troops. One of these groups wore "fire whisks," old symbols of the earth's creation, on their helmets. Today we know the symbol as a swastika; the Nazis would adopt it some years later.

At first, Hitler was not very involved in the politics or the chaos of Munich. His job as a soldier was mostly to test gas masks. But he soon became involved in politics, perhaps starting as a representative for his army unit. When the Red revolution was put down, Hitler quickly became known as an anti-communist and nationalist.

BLAMING GERMANY'S JEWS

At the time, the army played an important role in politics. Officers organized against the communists. Hitler began taking classes and attending lectures on German nationalism, economics, and other matters. He lectured other soldiers on the war and Germany's future. Among his common themes was the claim that Jews had caused Germany to lose the war. He said they were responsible for the "stab in the back."

Hitler discovered his talent as a speaker in Munich. The soldiers and others who listened to his lectures were greatly impressed. His ability to sway crowds grew quickly, until he ranked as one of the most influential speakers of all time.

Anti-Semitism was one of Hitler's main themes. It fit with his goal of making Germany strong again. A strong Germany must not be governed by communists or Jews, he insisted. It had to be racially pure. Germans had to turn away from the weakness and corruption of Jews and others. Hitler cited Jews as scapegoats. He blamed them for anything and everything bad. Jews were rich or Jews were vermin. Jews were capitalists or Jews were communists. Whatever Hitler wanted to denounce in a speech, he claimed it was Jewish.

In reality, Jewish Germans had served in the army in great numbers during World War I. As a group, Jews were no different than other German citizens. Some were very patriotic, others were not. Some were well-to-do, others were poor. The idea that Jews had stabbed Germany in the back was voiced again and again, but it was a lie. And yet, people applauded when Hitler said it. The idea was popular and widespread. Many Germans were looking for someone to blame. Jews had often been scapegoats in the past and were easy to attack now.

Historians have searched for many years for the exact moment at which Hitler became a rabid anti-Semite. Hitler's own statements point to Vienna, where he first read anti-Semitic literature. But many historians believe the pivotal moment occurred in Munich. They think that the experience of the failed communist revolt there was important to him. They also believe that the classes and lectures in which he took part played a role. It may be that the answer is very complicated and that no precise turning point existed. Hate is a simple emotion; learning to hate may be more complicated.

CHAPTER TWO

THE NSDAP

Besides making speeches to soldiers, Hitler's duties in the army also included spying on local political groups. On Friday, September 12, 1919, these duties brought Hitler to a meeting of the German Workers' Party. The party was one of several groups with similar aims. All wanted to return Germany to its former glory. They were opposed to communism, though they did back some socialist ideas.

When he first began spying on them, Hitler didn't think much of the German Workers' Party. However, he agreed with much of what the party leaders said. He also may have received support and encouragement from his army commander to join and strengthen the small party. At the time, nobody knew that the German Workers' Party would soon evolve into the Nazi Party. Nor is it likely that anyone would have predicted how infamous Hitler would become as the party's leader.

RISING IN THE PARTY

Hitler quickly became a popular party member. Not only could he speak very well to large groups, he was a superb organizer. Hitler remained in the army until March 1920, spending more and more time with the German Workers' Party. By the time of his discharge from the army, he was one of the party's best speakers and a key member.

Hitler tended to wear a loose-fitting suit jacket during his speeches. Usually these lasted two hours. He almost always talked of Germany's glorious past, contrasting it to the present chaos. The past he talked about was an idealized myth that hadn't actually existed, but it inspired the crowd. Hitler claimed that Jews and communists took advantage of Germans. They were the enemy. He criticized the agreement that ended World War I, which was imposing harsh conditions on Germany. And he promised a better future through nationalism and a return to old values like hard work.

As the German Workers' Party grew, its organization shifted. Its name changed to the National Socialist German Workers' Party or NSDAP. It was from this abbreviation that the word "Nazi" was derived because of the sound of the German letters. Hitler at first refused to be the party chairman. Conflicts with others led him to quit temporarily. But suddenly he began working hard to take

Hitler quickly became an important member of the Nazi Party. Here he is at a meeting of the party's paramilitary group, the SA, on Fröttmaning Heath, near Munich, in 1923.

over. In the summer of 1921, he became party's chairman, or "Führer."

GERMANY IN THE 1920S

At the end of World War I, the victorious allies imposed large fines, or reparations, on Germany. Raising money to pay them helped wreck the German economy. Even without them, the economy would have had a hard time recovering from the war. Businesses had closed. Many people did not have jobs.

A large number of unemployed people joined paramilitary organizations. These were called by many names, including the Freikorps, or "Free

Corps." Some local governments used paramilitary organizations to keep order. Others were sponsored by or aligned with political parties and acted like bodyguards for them. The Freikorps used violence to support political aims. They would attack opponents, for example, to enforce a boycott. They were even sometimes responsible for murder.

The Nazis had one such group of their own. They were called the Sturmabteilung, or "storm troopers." The Sturmabteilung—which is often abbreviated to SA—started as security officers for large meetings in the Munich beer halls. Like the other paramilitary groups, they were brutal when dealing with enemies.

By the end of 1921, the SA was headed by Ernst Röhm. Röhm would remain a close friend of Hitler's for the next decade. His efforts at organizing the SA were an important part of the Nazi Party's success. Like the rest of the party, the SA slowly increased in membership.

Things in Germany went from bad to worse during the early 1920s. The government failed to deliver some of the coal and wood that Germany owed as reparations. The French decided to retaliate. In January 1923, the French army occupied the Ruhr, an industrial section of Germany near the border with France. The German government began a campaign of passive resistance. That only made things worse. By the time the government finally gave in to the French, the economy was shattered. Prices escalated and money became worthless. Necessities like bread and milk cost millions of German marks. Life savings were wiped out. Many people wanted to overthrow the national and state governments. Revolutions and takeovers—called *"putsches,"* from a German word for a sudden or quick thrust—occurred in many parts of the country.

THE BEER HALL PUTSCH

Among those clamoring for a putsch were Nazi Party members in Munich. Hitler and other Nazis had been denouncing the city government for a long time. Their supporters wanted more than just criticism. They wanted action. On November 8, 1923, Hitler and the other Nazi leaders finally agreed. Several hundred SA and other party members armed themselves with machine guns and other weapons. They surrounded a beer hall in which prominent members of the city and state government were listening to a speech. The Nazis took them prisoner. Their aim was to take over the city and to eventually provoke an uprising against the national government, too.

In later years, Hitler would use glowing words to describe the putsch. In reality, it was an inept bungle. Hitler couldn't make up his mind

While the Beer Hall Putsch was pretty much a complete failure, Hitler and other leaders of the Nazi Party learned what not to do in the future.

exactly what to do once
the government officials
were taken prisoner. His
demands were muddled.
His supporters like Röhm
were just as disorganized.
In the meantime, the army
and state police remained
loyal to the government.
By 5:00 a.m. the next day,
it was obvious that their
revolution had failed.

Hitler and the Nazis
decided to march to the
center of the city. They
may have believed that the
citizens of the city would
join them. Or they may have
been unable to think of anything better to do. As they
marched, Hitler and several
other leaders at the front
of the group linked their
hands. There were roughly
two thousand party mem-
bers in the procession, many
armed with guns. One group
of policemen retreated as
they headed in the direction
of the Defense Ministry.
But the Nazis soon came up

against a second, larger group of policemen blocking the street. As they approached the barricades, the police began shooting. Nazi Party members threw themselves to the ground and then ran for their lives. Among those who ran away was Adolf Hitler.

Fourteen Nazi followers and four policemen were killed in the riot that ended the Beer Hall Putsch. Many more were wounded. Hitler dislocated his arm. He was arrested at the home where he had gone to have his injury treated. The police charged him with treason. He was convicted and sentenced to five years in prison. He would end up serving less than one year.

HITLER'S TRIAL

At his trial, Hitler was allowed to talk about his political beliefs. He tried to put the German government on trial. He called himself a "drummer" for the patriotic forces in Germany. Most Germans were not Nazis, but Hitler made the Nazis sound as if they were the nation's future leaders.

Hitler confessed to his actions, but he said they could not be considered treason.

He said that treason had been committed by the government in signing the armistice of November 1918. The "November criminals" were the ones who were guilty of treason. He spoke well. Many, including the judge, were on his side by the time the trial ended.

MEIN KAMPF

During his time in prison, Hitler began composing a book that was a messy mix of a memoir and a manifesto. He dictated much of it to fellow Nazi Party member Rudolph Hess. The book—named *Mein Kampf*, which means "My Suffering" in German—was published in two volumes, the first of which came out on July 18, 1925. In the book Hitler described his early life, went into great detail about his racist ideas, and laid out his plan for the Nazi movement and Germany in general.

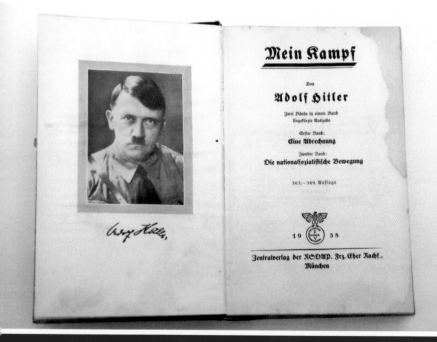

After Hitler came to power, several editions of *Mein Kampf* were published. This 1938 edition featured a photograph of the author on the frontispiece, or first page of the book.

While the book wasn't especially successful at the time of its publication, *Mein Kampf* eventually sold twelve million copies. In fact, once the Nazi Party came to power, the book became a popular present for German citizens to give each other in order to mark important life milestones, such as weddings or high school graduations. Historians doubt whether many of the Germans who owned the book actually read it in full, though, since *Mein Kampf* is long and confusingly written. Hitler may have been a best-selling writer, but he wasn't a very talented one.

CHAPTER THREE

THE NAZIS GAIN SUPPORT

By the time that Hitler was released from jail, the German economy had begun to improve. The Nazis, like many of the other small, fanatical parties, were losing support. People didn't feel quite as desperate. Hopeful about their own futures, they didn't fall for the messages of hate. Meanwhile, the failed putsch had damaged the Nazis' reputation. They looked like inept bunglers. The putsch and Hitler's imprisonment also caused dissension and disorganization within the Nazi Party. Members left for other groups or lost interest. Leaders feuded with each other.

After he was released from jail, Hitler devoted a great deal of his time to reorganizing the Nazi movement. He did not do this alone, of course. Among those who helped him were Hermann Göring, a World War I fighter pilot who had been wounded in the putsch. Another was Gregor Strasser. With his brother Otto, Gregor Strasser played an important role in the party, especially in Berlin. Hitler eventually split with the Strasser brothers—first with Otto, then with

Hermann Göring was a faithful follower of Hitler and an important Nazi leader. After World War II ended, he was tried, found guilty, and executed for war crimes and crimes against humanity.

Gregor. The conflict was partly over political philosophy. Otto leaned more toward socialism than Hitler did. But the conflict was also about power and popularity. During the early 1920s, Hitler increased his hold over the party. He was very good at outmaneuvering opponents and keeping underlings and allies off balance. Despite his disagreements with the Strassers, he was careful not to attack them directly while they were still powerful. Gregor Strasser remained an important party member through the 1920s. He was second only to Hitler.

HITLER'S LEADERSHIP STYLE

Hitler was also an excellent organizer, able to inspire other people to do hard work for the Nazi Party. Hitler himself did not spend long hours at a desk or in an office. He was capable of attending to many details and had an excellent memory. Hitler was very aware that a big part of his "job" was to create a larger-than-life image of a leader. He upheld this image always.

Hitler had a singular ability to make others feel important. People meeting him felt as if they were the center of his attention. He had tricks that helped him. One was a prolonged handshake. Another was a long stare into someone's eyes. Part of Hitler's success came from knowing what the other person expected. This indirect flattery and his personal

Joseph Goebbels, seen here meeting with Hitler at Berlin's Tempelhof Airport, led the Nazi's extensive propaganda efforts. Propaganda is biased information used to influence an audience's views.

charm were important weapons of persuasion. His temper was a powerful weapon as well.

Hitler's ideas and abilities led many people to worship him as a hero. One of the most important people who did so was Joseph Goebbels. Goebbels joined the Nazi Party around the time that Hitler was jailed. Though disabled with a club-foot, Goebbels was intelligent and an able speaker. He met Hitler for the first time around 1925. At first, Goebbels was an ally of Gregor Strasser. His political philosophy was nearer to Strasser's than it was to Hitler's. But Hitler won him over to his side. He did this through flattery and by giving him important party jobs. Goebbels, like many others, saw Hitler as a father figure for the country. He believed that Germany needed a strong leader and saw Hitler as that leader.

HYPNOTIC HITLER

Hitler had a special ability when speaking to large audiences. Some people who observed it compared it to hypnotism. His voice had a strident ring to it. With sharp gestures and rising emotions, Hitler could excite a crowd. His speeches could last for hours. They tended to follow simple themes that Hitler repeated over and over again:

Germany had been great.
Germany had been betrayed at the end of World War I.
The Jews and communists were responsible.

TAKING PART IN ELECTIONS

Hitler and the Nazis believed that democracy was a weak form of government. But the party still decided to participate in Germany's elections. Hitler stated that the Nazis would come to power legally. Some historians and biographers believe that the failed putsch taught him that armed force alone would never be enough to take power.

As hard as Hitler and others worked, the Nazis remained a small party through mid-1928. Like America in its Roaring Twenties, Germany was experiencing good economic times. But things were starting to change again at about the time the speaking ban was lifted on Hitler. The economy was already showing some signs of weakness. At the same time, Hitler's work at organizing the Nazis was starting to pay off.

In the May 1928 elections, the Nazi Party managed to elect twelve representatives to the country's parliament, which was called the Reichstag. Among the representatives were three very important Nazis: Göring, Goebbels, and Gregor Strasser. At first glance, the election results appeared disappointing. There were more than five hundred seats in the Reichstag. Many people interpreted the results as proof that the Nazis were insignificant. But the election was a sign of things to come. The Nazis' best results had come from voters who were suffering economically. Hitler and others recognized the trend. Instead of giving up, they worked harder than ever to get people to join their party.

On August 1, 1929, somewhere between thirty and forty thousand Nazi Party members, many of them also members of the SA, descended on the southern German city of Nuremberg. For four days, they filled the town and the stadium there with chants and slogans. The Nazi swastika was plastered everywhere. Hitler presided over it all, with carefully planned public appearances. Behind the scenes, small groups of Nazi Party leaders and organizers took their cue from him, laying out plans for the near future. It was now clear to everyone that the economy was turning sour. France and Britain were pushing for more reparations.

THE GREAT DEPRESSION

Soon after the Nazi Party congress in Nuremberg, the American stock market crashed. The crash was the final blow to the world economy. It had a sharp effect on Germany because the country had been using American loans to help keep things going. When those loans dried up, things in Germany got even worse.

Hitler exploited these bad times. He attacked the reparation plan. He repeated his message that the Nazis could save Germany. In some instances, he seemed to have softened his attacks on Jews, though he continued to use that we might call code words, such

Hitler gives the Nazi salute at the 1929 Nuremburg Rally. The Nazis held several huge rallies in Nuremberg. Aside from the one in 1929, there were ones in 1923, 1927, and every year between 1933 and 1938.

as "vermin" and "disease." Still, it was pretty clear that he and many other Nazis were deeply anti-Semitic.

The Nazis did well in state elections in 1929. In some cases, the number of votes that the party won in local elections doubled. More importantly, many young people joined the party. Their energy helped increase the Nazi Party's efforts. There were two main reasons why many people looked to the Nazis during hard times. First, they provided both a scapegoat and a solution—the Jews were the cause of the problem, and getting rid of them would lead to a grand future. Some people also saw the Nazis as a counterweight to the communists. Hitler's rhetoric was strongly anticommunist. Nazi SA members often fought Communist Party members in the streets.

THE TIDE TURNS

Hitler appointed Goebbels to organize the Nazi Party's campaign during the summer of 1930. It proved to be a brilliant stroke. Goebbels, who had headed the party in Berlin, was a master campaign manager. He organized speeches and party meetings all across the country. Handouts and newspapers were used to spread propaganda. Goebbels orchestrated SA demonstrations, fights, and riots to gain the party publicity.

Hitler gave speeches all across the country during the campaign's final weeks. He sensed that the party would do well. At one point he predicted that the Nazis would come to power by 1934. But probably not even Hitler could have predicted the outcome of the election. Instead of the 12 seats they had held, the Nazis ended up with 107. Approximately 6.5 million Germans had voted for the Nazis, making them the second largest party in the Reichstag. The Nazis, and Hitler, had arrived.

CHAPTER FOUR

CAMPAIGNING FOR POWER

After World War I, Germany was run by a president, a chancellor, and a parliament, called the Reichstag. An absolute majority could select the chancellor. The chancellor would then select ministers who would run the government. Whichever party controlled the Reichstag would select its leader as chancellor. But Germany had many parties in the Reichstag. None of them alone could get a majority. They had to compromise and work together. As time went on, differences in political philosophy and personality clashes made compromise impossible.

At the same time, the president of Germany had unusual power. Under the constitution, he could allow a chancellor to form a government without approval from the Reichstag. In other words, the president could say it was okay for a chancellor to rule without agreement in the Reichstag. Paul von Hindenburg, a former field marshal who held the presidency between 1925 and 1934, did this several times. He did it so often that it became the common way for the government to function. This divided the government

Paul von Hindenburg was so popular in Germany that Hitler chose not to remove him from office. He waited until Hindenburg's death in 1934 to eliminate the office of president.

and left the chancellor weak. It also distanced the public from the government.

The system worked until the economic problems of the late 1920s and early 1930s. Then the lack of cooperation between the parties made it impossible to agree on solutions. These disputes also meant that an unusual number of Reichstag elections were held. Dissolving the government and calling for new elections was one way to try and find a majority. It ended up helping the Nazis.

TO RUN OR NOT TO RUN

By 1932, Hitler was debating over whether to run for president of Germany. Everyone knew that Hindenburg, the incumbent president, would win. But the Nazis' impressive victories during the recent Reichstag elections made it important for them to challenge Hindenburg. If they didn't, their gains might be lost.

On the other hand, if the candidate lost badly, they'd be finished. The only person in the party who was well-known enough to challenge Hindenburg was Hitler. But it was a very risky move. Goebbels and other important Nazis convinced Hitler it was worth the gamble. While Hindenburg was very popular, many candidates were running for president. They would divide up the votes. Hitler's supporters, however, were likely to remain loyal. That would give him a strong base. Not enough to win, maybe, but enough to finish strongly. He might even force a runoff or second election. It would make Hitler look like an important leader.

Goebbels was right. When the votes were counted, Hitler finished second with roughly 30 percent of the vote. This helped force a second election with only three candidates. Besides Hitler and Hindenburg, there was a third candidate, Ernst Thalmann, who was a communist.

Campaigning in the runoff election was even more furious. Hitler delivered twenty speeches in roughly a week's time. Goebbels and thousands of other party leaders, speakers, and members worked just as hard. As expected, Hitler lost to Hindenburg in

Hitler gave many campaign speeches in 1932. Here he is addressing a crowd at the Berlin Sportpalast, a winter sports arena in Berlin.

GELI RAUBAL

While Hitler liked being with women, there is little evidence that he had any love affairs until after World War I. And the few relationships he had with women during the 1920s and early 1930s seem to have been superficial. There was one exception—Geli Raubal. Geli was the daughter of Hitler's half-sister, Angela Raubal. They met during the summer of 1925, when Hitler was staying at a house in Berchtesgarten in the Bavarian Alps. At the time, Geli was seventeen. In 1929, she moved to his apartment in Munich.

While Hitler seems to have been emotionally attached to Geli, historians are not sure their relationship was sexual. Geli flirted openly with other men and may have had an affair with Hitler's chauffeur. Hitler gradually became jealous and more controlling. By the fall of 1931, Geli wanted to leave Hitler. The reason is unclear. She may have found a new boyfriend, or she may have simply wanted to be out of her uncle's control. Whatever the case, she was clearly unhappy with their relationship.

On September 18, 1931, Hitler left Munich for Nuremberg. The next morning he received word that Geli had been found dead in his apartment, his pistol by her side. The death was declared a suicide, though that didn't stop rumors from spreading.

the runoff election. But he polled 37 percent of the vote. This was more than had been predicted. Over a third of the German electorate had now voted for Hitler and his party at least once. But the hard work and campaigning of 1932 was just beginning. After the presidential election, local and state elections were held in late April. That meant another round of fierce campaigning. Again, Hitler flew all over the country. Again, the Nazis did well. The party started planning for the new Reichstag elections set for the end of July.

DISAGREEMENT IN THE REICHSTAG

The July 1932 Reichstag elections were a great victory for the Nazis. They won 230 seats. They were now the largest party in the Reichstag. But the victory proved frustrating. They weren't large enough to select a chancellor on their own. And they couldn't find another party to work with.

Hindenburg and other political leaders refused to make Hitler chancellor. They didn't want him to head the government. Hitler refused compromises that would have given him or other party members less important roles in the cabinet. He wanted to be number one, or he didn't want to be involved. He thought Hindenburg would give in. He was wrong. A new government was formed without the Nazis— and then dissolved. Hitler felt defeated. He had

These members of the Nazi Party are waiting to be sworn in by Hitler after the party's sweeping victory in the July 31, 1932, election.

failed to achieve the powerful position in government that he wanted.

In the fall elections, the Nazi Party didn't do quite as well as it had during the summer. Hitler's party got about 33 percent of the vote but lost more than thirty seats. Still, they continued to be the biggest party in the Reichstag, with 196 representatives. Once again, no party had an absolute majority, no coalition could be formed, and the president stepped in to choose a chancellor. Hitler continued to maneuver. He tried to convince Hindenburg to select him. He offered to accept cabinet members from outside the Nazi Party. But Hindenburg held firm against him. He appointed Kurt von Schleicher chancellor.

Schleicher tried to split the Nazis by getting

Gregor Strasser to take the position of vice chancellor. Hitler reacted quickly, calling on subordinates and personally speaking to Nazi Party members across the country to cement his support. He asserted himself with diplomacy and skill, using all of his talents as an organizer and a persuader. Strasser quickly realized that he was in no position to challenge Hitler and resigned from the Nazi Party.

Schleicher soon lost Hindenburg's support. The president began looking for a new chancellor. At first, he favored naming a past chancellor, Franz von Papen. Papen was an aristocrat with important family and business connections. He was a centrist politician, though he had split with other members of his party, the Center Party. But it soon became clear that Papen couldn't get enough support.

PAPEN'S DEAL

Papen then put together a deal to have Hitler named chancellor, with himself as vice chancellor. The Nazis would have only a limited number of seats in the new cabinet. One key to the deal was an alliance between the conservative German National Party and the Nazis, which Papen managed to arrange.

Historians have debated why Hindenburg agreed to the deal. Some point out that Hitler and the Nazis seemed weakened by the November election. Some feel this meant that Hindenburg should have ignored Hitler. Others think that it gave Hindenburg the impression that he had less reason to fear Hitler. A few believe that Hitler and the Nazis had found embarrassing information about a land deal and were blackmailing Hindenburg. Others say that Hindenburg, who had been born in 1847 and was now in his eighties, was senile and simply gave in to the arguments of people he trusted, including his son.

Whatever Hindenburg's reasons, the Nazis enjoyed strong support throughout the country. At the same time, German leaders like Papen clearly underestimated Hitler. They may not have taken him or his movement seriously enough. Papen told other conservatives that he would "push Hitler into a corner," according to historian Henry Ashby Turner. Hitler's hateful ideas about Jews and his attacks against democracy were clearly expressed in his speeches. The history of the Nazi Party demonstrated that Hitler would not hesitate to use violence to reach his goals. If anyone in the country didn't believe he would try to put these ideas into practice, they were very, very mistaken.

Schleicher was forced to resign as chancellor on January 28, 1933. On the night of January 29, Hitler gathered with Göring and other Nazi leaders at Goebbels's house in Berlin. He had concluded the deal with Papen, but the army's

The Nazis' rise to power, and Hitler's rise to chancellor, happened over the course of just a few years.

opinion was unknown. The final lineup of the cabinet still hadn't been set. Hitler spent a sleepless night, worrying about what might go wrong. However he didn't have to worry. The next morning, Hitler, Göring and other Nazis joined Papen and other conservative politicians at the Reich Chancellery. They argued in the room outside the president's office over some last-minute details, but, in the end, Hitler was shown in to the president and was sworn in as chancellor.

CHAPTER FIVE

DICTATORSHIP

About a month after Hitler came to power in 1933, the Reichstag building was set on fire. Hitler and others claimed that the fire was set as part of a communist conspiracy. They then used the fire as an excuse to ban the communists and some other left-wing members from the Reichstag. With them out, the Nazis voted themselves more power. The law giving Hitler expanded power was called the Enabling Act. This law helped make Hitler a legal dictator.

The Nazis threatened legislators and pressured them to vote for the act. Many representatives felt they were bullied into supporting it. Even so, the law and Hitler were popular with the people. As time went on, there was less and less opposition in the Reichstag. In some cases, parties that might have opposed the Nazis were either banned or intimidated. In other cases, interest in those parties dwindled due to the Nazis' popularity. Communists were persecuted. Some were imprisoned; a few were killed. Many wisely fled for their lives. In the meantime, Hitler continued to consolidate his power.

Though he is now a hated figure, Hitler was tremendously popular in Germany during the 1930s and early 1940s. These crowds are cheering for him at the 1937 Nuremburg Rally.

CRACKING DOWN ON THE SA

On June 30, 1934, Hitler stomped down the hallway of a hotel, sweeping into a small room. Ernst Röhm, the head of the SA, lay sleeping in a bed.

"Röhm, you're under arrest," thundered Hitler. He snapped his rhino-hide riding crop against his leg. Röhm, half asleep, tried to ask Hitler what was going on.

"You're under arrest!" shouted the Führer, spinning on his heel and leaving Röhm to the officers he'd brought with him on this hot summer night. It was the last time he would see his former friend alive.

Röhm's arrest was part of a crackdown against the SA. Many men aside from Röhm—perhaps as many as four hundred—were murdered during this crackdown. The action removed the greatest threat to Hitler's control of the country. Ironically, that threat came from some of his closest supporters

Before the crackdown on the SA, Ernst Röhm had been a top Nazi leader. Here, Röhm inspects SA soldiers on parade.

and oldest friends—the illegal army that had helped bring him to power.

The SA had grown in power along with Hitler and the rest of the Nazi Party. It had increased in size and was well armed. It had set up concentration camps to punish its enemies. These were the precursors of the death camps used later to exterminate Jews and others. With its size and power growing, Nazi leaders realized that the SA might someday be strong enough to overthrow the government. The army also saw the SA as a serious threat. Hitler needed the army's backing to govern, so this presented continual problems.

For months, Hitler debated how to deal with Röhm. Some steps were taken. Control of the concentration camps was eventually taken away from the SA leadership. But Hitler's fear that the SA would turn against him grew. There were rumors that a putsch or coup was being planned. Many SA members were angry that the German economy had not improved fast enough. Röhm had been with Hitler from the early days of the struggle. Hitler liked him and felt loyal to him. And with perhaps hundreds of thousands of men ready to follow him, curbing Röhm was a delicate matter.

Hitler had reason to fear Röhm and the SA. Many storm troopers seemed to be disillusioned or disappointed in the Nazi Party. The SA had included the most violent and radical members of the party. Many of them worried that the Nazi leadership was moving too slowly.

Prodded by leaders like Heinrich Himmler and Göring, Hitler finally decided to act. He may have believed false documents that indicated the SA was planning a coup. Or he may have known the documents were fake. In any event, he worked himself into a rage and supervised the arrests. Several other political enemies, including Gregor Strasser, were killed in the purge.

MAINTAINING CONTROL

It may seem odd that the greatest threat to Hitler's power was from his friends. By the summer of 1934, though, Hitler had managed to eliminate or outmaneuver his other opponents. The Nazi leader had increased his hold on power in several ways. Sometimes he used intimidation and threats. Often, however, his methods were democratic and at least technically legal.

Hitler increased his control of the government and police by moving Nazi Party members into important positions. Since he had absolute control of the party, he could exert his control through party members. His popularity also helped tremendously. Many people, even those who didn't vote for him, liked Hitler and wanted him to succeed. As Hindenburg grew older and sicker, his influence gradually decreased. In some ways, President Hindenburg had been a check on the Nazis. The less important he was, the more important Hitler became.

A POPULAR DICTATOR

Today, we think of dictators as harsh leaders whom everyone hates. But Hitler was actually loved by many people. How could a dictator be popular? For one thing, Hitler avoided the conflicts that had crippled earlier German governments. Most members of the Nazi Party worked together. His dictatorial ways brought order to the government.

The improving economy was an even more important reason for Hitler's popularity. The entire world, including Germany, was in a major depression. Many people were without jobs. Wages remained low and food prices high. But Hitler's government made things better. People felt optimistic about the future.

Nazi propaganda, which was organized by Joseph Goebbels, was another reason. It always showed Hitler in the best light. It didn't hurt that Hitler stood up to England and France. Many people felt that the two nations were trying to bully Germany. By reinstating the draft and disregarding the Versailles Treaty, Hitler told his enemies that Germany would not be pushed around. This made Germans feel good about themselves and their country. Millions joined the Nazi Party.

On August 2, 1934, the 86-year-old Hindenburg died. Hitler took over as president as well as chancellor. He had achieved his goal; he was absolute dictator. He was also extremely popular.

PERSECUTING JEWS

Once in power, the Nazis took several steps against Jews. On April 1, 1933, Goebbels and other Nazis organized a boycott of Jewish businesses. It was a failure. Many Germans simply ignored it. Others complained about SA violence against Jews. The boycott quickly ended, but anti-Semitic propaganda and persecution continued. Jews were beaten on the street. Laws were passed greatly restricting Jewish life.

In 1935, the Nazi-controlled Reichstag instituted the Nuremberg Laws. The most important of these laws stripped Jews of their legal rights as citizens. Basically, the law declared that Jews were enemies of Germany. It provided legal grounds not only to discriminate against Jews, but also to take their property—and their lives. Roughly a quarter of the Jewish population left Germany between 1933 and 1937. And then things got even worse.

In November 1938, high-ranking Nazis organized a countrywide "action" against Jews. Assaults against Jews and their property were carefully planned. Stores were smashed and many Jewish people were arrested and taken to concentration camps. The action became known as Kristallnacht—which means "Crystal Night" or the "Night of Broken Glass." Kristallnacht and the Nuremberg Laws made it clear that Hitler was serious about making Germany "pure" by getting rid of the Jews, who he had declared *Untermenschen*, or a racially inferior group. More Jews fled Germany after Kristallnacht. But it soon became very difficult for them to do so.

Today, historians debate exactly how anti-Semitic Germans were when Hitler came to power. Some believe that pressure from radical SA members and other Nazis led to the passage of the Nuremberg Laws. They point out that Hitler sometimes toned down his attacks. Some remind us that others besides Hitler shared the blame for the violence against Jews. Still, it is clear that Hitler saw the Jews as a cancer that had to be removed from Germany. At any rate, the widespread violence

The name Kristallnacht comes from all the broken glass that resulted when SA members and mobs of German citizens attacked Jewish-owned stores, homes, and synagogues.

against the country's Jewish population could not have continued without his approval.

EXPANDING GERMANY

Besides purifying the German race, Hitler had another major goal—restoring the borders of "Greater Germany" and then adding "living space" in the east. This meant taking over Austria and parts of other countries where ethnic Germans lived. It also meant invading countries to the east, like Poland and the Soviet Union, and using them as colonies.

Hitler began working toward this goal by expanding the military. This was a violation of the Treaty of Versailles. Hitler went even further in March 1936, when he marched troops into the Rhineland. Though this was German territory, it bordered France. Placing troops in this area was forbidden under the treaty. Though his army was still weak, Hitler gambled that the French would do nothing. He was right. "Had the French marched into the Rhineland," he later said, "we would have had to withdraw." It set the stage for annexing Austria and Czechoslovakia.

Like Hitler, many Austrians considered themselves German rather than Austrian. But Austria included people who were not ethnic Germans. And even many of those who were ethnically German did not want to unite with Germany. Hitler encouraged Austrian Nazis to campaign for Austria's annexation.

He worked diplomatically to bring the countries together. He also threatened Austria with his army. As the Austrian government resisted, he stepped up pressure. Finally, in early 1938, he ordered German troops to prepare an invasion. There was a great deal of pressure on the Austrians. Not only was there a large German army on their border, but also many Austrians were demonstrating in favor of the Nazis. Finally, the government complied.

The Nazis referred to the takeover of Austria as the Anschluss, which means "union." Hitler's entry into Vienna, seen here, was greeted by cheering crowds.

On March 12, 1938, Hitler crossed the Austrian border to visit his birthplace at Braunau am Inn. Victory made him bolder. Within a month and a half, he mapped out a plan for similar action against Czechoslovakia. This time, Great Britain and France tried to stop Hitler. They seemed ready to go to war. Hitler felt it was a bluff, but his generals didn't. They might even have planned to overthrow Hitler if war started. But if so, they never got the chance. As Hitler had calculated, Great Britain and France were not prepared to go to war against Germany over Czechoslovakia. They reached an agreement that gave part of the country to Germany without a fight. British prime minister Neville Chamberlain declared that the negotiations had guaranteed "peace in our time." In reality, this weakness only made Hitler bolder.

CHAPTER SIX

CONQUERING EUROPE

Germany began World War II with the invasion of Poland in September 1939. German airplanes, tanks, and soldiers swept quickly into the country. A new word was invented to describe the quickness of the attack: "blitzkrieg," or lightning war.

The steps leading to the invasion were similar to those Hitler had used against Austria and Czechoslovakia. But this time Great Britain and France declared war on Germany. They had finally decided to take Hitler seriously. Even so, the French and British armies took little action against the Germans at first. Within a month, Germany controlled most of Poland. The Soviet Union invaded eastern Poland at the same time. The Soviets had a secret agreement with the Germans to split the country.

Hitler's invasion of Poland was extremely popular in Germany. Many Germans felt it was rightfully theirs. The conquest also brought riches to many Germans. They were able to set up businesses in the occupied territory and make a great deal of money. But above all, the easy victories in Austria, Czechoslovakia, and Poland made Hitler popular because they were just that—easy victories. Few Germans had been killed. At the same time, German territory had been greatly expanded.

THE INVASION OF WESTERN EUROPE

The German army invaded Denmark and Norway on April 10, 1940. Within six hours the small country of Denmark surrendered, its leaders convinced that they could not drive back the German forces that far outnumbered the Danish army. In Norway, several key ports fell to the Germans in the first day of fighting. However, the occupation of the capital, Oslo, met with delays, which allowed the royal family and members of the government to escape. Allied forces arrived to drive out the Germans and the fighting continued into June, by which point the Allies were preoccupied elsewhere.

On May 10, Hitler's armies began sweeping the Netherlands, Belgium, Luxembourg, and France. Eighty-nine divisions—including ten Panzer, or tank, divisions—led the charge. Relying on better weapons and training as well as surprise, the Germans moved quickly. By June 14, Paris had fallen. The French government surrendered a few days later.

The German army made plans to invade Great Britain. The Luftwaffe, or German air force,

The Nazi invasion of Belgium began on May 10, 1940. Though British troops arrived to support the Belgian army, the German onslaught was strong and the Belgian king surrendered on May 28.

launched a massive bombing campaign against England. Civilian as well as military targets were hit. However, Britain's Royal Air Force proved more formidable than Hitler had foreseen, and the British people refused to surrender. At any rate, Hitler's chief aim remained the one he had proclaimed years before in *Mein Kampf*: living space in the East. That meant Russia. As the idea of invading England faded, the army began moving its troops eastward.

LEADING THE ARMY

Hitler had been a corporal in World War I. While that gave him a lot of practical experience, it did not train him to lead armies. Nor had he studied strategy or tactics. Nevertheless he played an important role in leading the German military. Besides setting general policy, he understood new weapons and military technology. He made sure the army generals had new weapons and pushed them to use these weapons effectively. German tanks and large artillery pieces were developed on his direct orders. As the war went on, he influenced and directed battle strategy and tactics.

Historians have debated how good a general Hitler was. His abilities are difficult to assess, however, since the army won great victories and suffered terrible defeats because of his decisions. It is clear, however, that he considered his role as military commander part of his job as Führer. He believed that his political goals called for military victory. He also believed that he was the only one who could achieve them. While this made him bold as a general, it also made him stubborn. He was unwilling to retreat at times when it would have been wise to do so.

THE INVASION OF THE USSR

In the dawn of June 22, 1941, German troops launched an attack on the Soviet Union. They were the spearhead of a massive army numbering over a million men, with more than 3,500 tanks and 2,700 airplanes. It was the largest army ever assembled. For several weeks, the German troops were as successful as any army in history. By November, they stood 50 miles (80 kilometers) from the gates of Moscow, the Soviet capital.

But as the cold, gray skies of Russia began to fill with snowflakes, the German advance stalled. The change in the weather signaled a change in German fortunes. The army was not properly equipped or trained for winter battle. More importantly, the army faced a massive enemy. Despite the Russians' early losses, their army was well motivated. The soldiers were protecting their homes and families. The Russian population was larger than the German population. Once the Soviet army could be reorganized and supplied, it would be a powerful force. But this lay ahead. In the fall of 1941, the German army consolidated its victories. The Germans dug in and made defensive posts as the winter came on.

While the German army was making its way toward Moscow, another group of Germans were busy behind the lines. Special units known as Einsatzgruppen had followed the army into Russia. Directed by the SS (Schutzstaffel, the guard unit of the Nazi Party), and the Gestapo (the brutal police unit within the SS), these groups were actually death squads. Their targets were both Jews and Soviet officials and Communist Party members in

The German invasion of the Soviet Union was known by the code name Operation Barbarossa. A horse-drawn baggage train accompanied these German troops as they advanced into the USSR.

the occupied territory. As living space was acquired, Hitler's other great goal—ridding Europe of Jews— would also be achieved.

THE ESTABLISHMENT OF NAZI CAMPS

After the invasion of Poland, the Germans took steps to separate the Jews from the rest of the population. Jewish people were forced to move to ghettos, or parts of cities with concentrated Jewish populations. Ghettos had already existed in many cities, but the Germans were methodical in funneling the Jewish population into an increasingly smaller number of ghettos. Jewish people from Germany and Austria were sent east to live in these eastern European ghettos. The idea was to gather the Jewish population into a few places so it was easier to control them—and would eventually be easier to kill them. Conditions in the ghettoes were very bad. The ghettos were crowded and dirty, and there was not enough food to go around. Many people died of disease and starvation, while others were killed by the Einsatzgruppen. By early 1942, the Germans had begun to liquidate the ghettos, sending the people living there to the Nazi camps.

The Nazis set up a number of different kinds of camps. The earliest kind of camp was the concentration camp. These were set up to act as prisons for people who were considered enemies of the state. The first regular concentration camp—Dachau, which was outside of Munich—was set up in 1933. In the early years, most of the people held there were political prisoners. In time, Jews, gay people, Jehovah's Witnesses, and Roma (often called

Gypsies) were also held there. Conditions in concentration camps were horrible. There was harsh discipline and bad living conditions. Scientists carried out unethical—and frequently painful or deadly—experiments on prisoners in some of the camps.

The first concentration camps had been in Germany itself, but, after the invasion of Poland, the Nazis began to build camps there, too. Around this

The people imprisoned in Nazi concentration camps lived in terrible conditions and faced brutal treatment. These starving prisoners were held at Dachau.

time, forced labor took on a bigger role in most of the camps. Camps from this time are sometimes referred to as forced-labor camps to differentiate them from the concentration camps of the 1930s. The Germans also required forced labor from the people in their POW (or prisoner-of-war) camps, as well as from the inhabitants of the ghettos. While forced labor sometimes consisted of manufacturing supplies for the German army, it could also be deliberately humiliating and pointless. Under the German "annihilation through work" program, certain groups of prisoners—such as Jews and Roma—were forced to work in conditions that would eventually lead to sickness and injury, and eventually death.

The first death camp was Chelmno, in central Poland. It opened in December 1941. Death camps, which are also known as extermination camps and killing centers, had a single purpose: the systematic death of the Jews and other people who the Germans saw as deserving of extermination. Some of the people who were sent to these death camps were shot, but the majority were killed in poison gas chambers. The killing centers were top secret, so the victims' bodies were burned to eliminate the evidence of the deaths. Between March 1942 and November 1943, more than 1.5 million Jews were killed at Belzec, Sobibor, and Treblinka, the three camps that made up the Operation Reinhard killing centers. By late 1943, the Germans began to shut these death

These Jewish women and children are being deported from the Warsaw ghetto to the Treblinka death camp. The Nazis presented the deportations as the Judenausseidlung, or "Jewish resettlement."

camps down and cover up the evidence of their existence. However, the Germans continued to send people to Auschwitz-Birkenau, in southern Poland. It was the biggest killing center and was part of a larger camp complex. More than a million people would die there.

CHAPTER SEVEN

HITLER'S ROLE IN THE HOLOCAUST

There has been much debate over the years about who deserves to be held responsible for the Holocaust. While historians agree that, as the leader of Nazi Germany, Hitler ultimately bears responsibility for the Holocaust, they still are not sure exactly how involved he was in working out the details of the genocide. There are also questions about the degree to which other people deserve to share in the blame.

THE FINAL SOLUTION

The Nazis used the term "Final Solution" to refer to their plans for the destruction of the Jewish people. While anti-Jewish rhetoric had been part of the Nazi movement at the beginning, what Göring referred to as "complete solution of the Jewish question" seems not to have been worked out until World War II was well underway.

We will probably never understand why Hitler did the horrendous things that he did. The debates over how much guilt others bear for the Holocaust are unlikely to end either.

Among the questions historians have is when the decision to murder the Jews was made. Did it evolve slowly? Did Hitler and others plan it from the first day they took power? Many historians today think that the plan to murder millions of Jews evolved over the years. They point out that while Hitler and the Nazis were anti-Semitic from the very beginning, organized mass murder did not start until the invasion of Russia. Other historians note that many Jews were killed before that. During the last months of 1941 and the early months of 1942, actions against Jews became more severe. It was only then that mass deportations and exterminations began, so many historians believe that the decision to approve mass murder happened then.

But if Hitler had always wanted to eliminate the Jews from Europe, why did he wait until the end of 1941 or the beginning of 1942? There are several possible answers. One is that while Hitler wanted to eliminate all Jews, he didn't have a chance to do so until then.

It is also possible that Hitler and the other important Nazis waited until they felt the public would not protest—a euthanasia program that the Nazis had tried earlier to kill the mentally ill had been strongly criticized. Hitler may have decided to act because he was worried the war would turn against Germany. On the other hand, he may have thought the war was going so well that it was time to act against the Jews.

EVIDENCE OF HITLER'S GUILT

As Joseph Goebbels returned to his office on an early December evening in 1941, he thought about Hitler's latest action. Goebbels himself had been pushing for it for many years. He sat at the desk and began to dictate his diary entry. He had been keeping the journal for years, recording his thoughts on politics, Germany, and Hitler. All of the great events of the Nazi Party were recorded there. There was nothing different or special about that day's entry. It was a matter of simple fact:

> *The Führer has decided to make a clean sweep. He told the Jews that if they again brought about a world war, they would be annihilated. That wasn't a slogan. The war is here.*

Hitler himself never wrote down his thoughts about the Holocaust and how it should be carried out. He usually did not issue orders on paper. He spoke to his underlings and expected them to carry out his orders. There are many records and much evidence relating to the actual murders themselves. But the decision-making process that led to them remains unclear.

The lack of a document from Hitler has led some to speculate that he was not actually involved in the Final Solution. But it is ludicrous to believe

HOLOCAUST DENIERS

Despite the fact that there is a wealth of evidence proving that the terrible events of the Holocaust really did happen, there continues to be a small group of people—known as Holocaust deniers—who argue that the Holocaust either did not happen, that the number of people who died is hugely overstated, or that there was no official Nazi policy demanding the extermination of the Jews. Many of these people are driven by nothing more than anti-Semitism. Holocaust deniers often point to the lack of documents directly tying Hitler to the Holocaust as evidence of their far-fetched claims.

In actuality, the lack of documentary evidence isn't that surprising. For one thing, Hitler frequently gave oral rather than written orders. More importantly, the Nazis had been very secretive about the "Final Solution" from the beginning. The mass deaths were concealed from the general public. Even during the war, the Nazis attempted to deliberately destroy evidence of the Holocaust. They dug up bodies in mass graves, crushing and burning the human remains before reburying them. They demolished Treblinka, Sobibor, and Belzec, planting trees and farm fields over the sites of the camps. When they abandoned Auschwitz near the end of the war, they destroyed all the records there.

that the Holocaust could have started and continued without his approval. Goebbels's diary entry is only one of the proofs that Hitler ordered the Holocaust. Historians have notes from Heinrich Himmler, the head of the SS, from around the same time. Historians also know when certain meetings about the Final Solution took place and when Hitler was visited by people involved in the murders. We probably will never know all the details about Hitler's decision. We only know what happened: millions of Jews were rounded up and shipped to death camps.

SHARED GUILT

It's not easy to kill eight million people. The Einsatzgruppen worked mostly with machine guns and some special gas vans. While they killed thousands upon thousands of people, it was soon clear how difficult mass executions were going to be. Killing millions required an assembly line of death. Jews had to be collected in ghettos and concentration camps. Railroads needed to be made available for transport. New methods of killing had to be perfected. Corpses had to be disposed of.

Thousands of Germans and other Europeans
were involved in the Holocaust. Not all were Nazis.
Historians have recently begun to reexamine what

Tens of thousands of people served as guards in Nazi camps. These guards served in the SS at Mauthausen concentration camp in Austria.

ordinary people did during the Holocaust. While a few helped save Jews, most did not. Even before Jews were shipped en masse to their deaths, they were persecuted in Germany. They had to wear badges that showed they were Jews. They worked as slaves for the war effort. They had no rights and were robbed of property. Few non-Jewish Germans protested these measures.

That does not lessen Hitler's responsibility. He raged against Jews in his first political speeches. He was the dictator of the country. He was the director and catalyst of the Holocaust. He created the atmosphere and the mechanism for death. He made it happen.

CHAPTER EIGHT

HITLER'S FINAL DAYS

By mid-1944, the western Allies were pushing Germany back from the Mediterranean, France, and Russia. Military analysts usually call Hitler's decision to invade the Soviet Union his key blunder of the war. The vast country and its harsh weather made it difficult to conquer. On the other hand, the German army had defeated Russian armies during World War I. Because of that history and Hitler's aim of acquiring living space in the East, his attack against the Soviet Union would have seemed logical to him.

The Eastern Front slowly drained the German armies. Hitler often commanded his generals to hold ground at all cost. Even when they were successful, they suffered massive losses. The Germans suffered on other fronts, but the steady attack by the Red Army from late 1941 onward set the stage for Germany's defeat. Besides the men and materials lost there, the action against Russia drained energy and attention from other areas.

The American and British invasion of France in June 1944 sealed Germany's fate.

A massive counterattack planned by Hitler that December won only a brief respite. As the winter began to give way to spring, troops closed in on Berlin from all directions.

HITLER IN DENIAL

The generals arriving at Hitler's command bunker at Berchtesgarten in the German Alps wore serious, worried looks. The Americans and British had landed in France earlier in the month. Already they were threatening to break through the defenses. Paris was in danger. The German forces were worn down. Even Field Marshall Erwin Rommel, the national hero who had won great victories earlier, feared the war would be lost. On the Eastern Front, things were even worse. The Soviet army had broken through the middle of the German lines. The way to Berlin was open.

The generals had been called together to discuss the situation in Hitler's underground command center. Caverns and tunnels gave way to large rooms here. Hitler's private quarters had been drilled into solid rock. The Führer's mood was dark. He listened to the hints that the German army should retreat and perhaps surrender. Coldly, he told the generals Germany would not give up. Then he launched into a long speech about special weapons being developed. Pilotless bombs would drop from the sky. Speedy jet fighters would swarm overhead. Hitler

Even as others began to doubt that they could win the war, Hitler continued to insist that Germany would emerge victorious.

shouted that the failures of his generals at the front would be overcome. The Reich would survive. The generals listened in disbelief.

The secret weapons that Hitler talked about did exist. But the situation was far worse than he admitted, at least to his generals. Germany was on the brink of losing the war. Meanwhile, Hitler's own health was deteriorating. It is difficult to know now whether this was due to the pressures of the war or a medical condition. Historians say that Hitler's doctor was a quack. He treated him for real and imagined ailments with drugs that were either useless or harmful. Historian H. R. Trevor-Roper says that the drugs included strychnine and belladonna, powerful poisons. There were also narcotics and stimulants. Though in his mid-fifties, Hitler looked much older. His left arm and leg trembled at times. He also had severe stomach cramps and gas.

LOSING FAITH IN HITLER

As the war continued to go badly, Hitler and other Nazi leaders punished dissent. Penalties were increased by transferring cases to Nazi Party courts. Anyone important who disagreed publicly with Hitler's policies risked prison or worse. When a state official named Theodor Korselt suggested that Hitler ought to step down, he was accused of undermining military morale and sentenced to death.

Most people kept silent, but the support Hitler had enjoyed in the 1930s had eroded. Several generals who attended the conferences at Hitler's headquarters wanted to overthrow the Führer. They realized Hitler wouldn't surrender and feared total annihilation. The only solution was to remove him.

Several attempts had been made to kill Hitler. According to biographer Joachim C. Fest, a time bomb had been placed on his plane in 1943 but failed to go off. Other plots had either been poorly planned or hampered by bad luck. In no case was a serious, coordinated coup carried out.

With the war going badly, some German generals and other officers decided to kill Hitler. They hoped that after Hitler was killed, others would join them. They plotted to kill the Führer and take over the government. Then they would make peace with the Allies.

In mid-July, Hitler traveled to his headquarters in East Prussia. Colonel Claus von Stauffenberg attended a conference there on July 20. Hitler and two dozen officers were gathered in a room around a large, oak table when Stauffenberg entered. He put down his briefcase and then quickly left, pretending he had to make a phone call. A few minutes later, the briefcase exploded. The walls and ceiling crashed in. Hitler was burned and his arm paralyzed. His back was injured by a beam, and his ears were harmed by the explosion. But he survived. Calmly, he gave orders to arrest the conspirators.

Claus von Stauffenberg fought in the German army during World War II. Troubled by the atrocities that the Germans were committing, he started making plans to overthrow Adolf Hitler in 1942.

Stauffenberg and others who had helped him were quickly captured. The conspirators had planned to use army units stationed in Berlin to take over the city. Their putsch was quickly and easily overcome. Hitler moved swiftly against the officers and civilians who had been involved in the plot. Just under five thousand people were executed. Thousands of others were sent to concentration camps or punished in other ways. Many were actually unconnected with the attempt, but Hitler and other Nazis used it as an excuse to remove enemies.

General Rommel had spoken with the conspirators before the bomb attack. It is possible that he would have joined the putsch. However, he had been injured in an Allied attack a few days before. He was in the hospital when the bomb went off.

Hitler gave Rommel a choice: stand trial or commit suicide. If he committed suicide, his family would be spared. Rommel chose suicide. Hitler honored his side of the bargain. Rommel had done him a great favor. Hitler would not have to admit that the country's most popular general had turned against him.

THE DEATH MARCHES

The Holocaust continued despite the German losses. As the Russians threatened to overrun the death camps in Poland and eastern Europe, SS troops dismantled them. Orders were given to hide the

The Soviet army reached Auschwitz on January 27, 1945. While the army was able to liberate several thousand prisoners, including these men, more than a million others had already been killed there.

evidence of the mass murders. Jews were taken from occupied countries and shipped to death centers to be exterminated even as Germany collapsed. When camps were too close to the front, the Jews there were marched deeper into Nazi territory. It is impossible to know exactly how many Jews and others were killed during the Holocaust. While the death toll among Jews is usually given as around 6 million, estimates of Jewish deaths range from 4.5 million to 8 million. By any count, the crime was immense.

HITLER'S DEATH

Underground headquarters had been built beneath the Chancellery building in Berlin. As the Allies closed in during the early months of 1945, Hitler retreated there with a few friends and government officials. Military planning continued in the bunker. But it had less and less to do with reality. Hitler's orders

NO SURRENDER

Surrender was impossible for Hitler. Hitler knew the Allies would never accept any deal that kept him in power. They were likely to execute him if they captured him. Surrender would mean nothing less than utter defeat for both Hitler and his "vision" for Germany.

Despite the continued losses, Hitler kept fighting. He knew that secret weapons were being developed. He saw that the western and eastern Allies were divided. He remembered that he had won great victories before when all seemed lost. He also believed that Germany had lost World War I only because its leaders had given up. It is impossible to say whether he truly believed that things would turn around. At some points toward the end of the war, he seems not to have understood how badly things were going. At other times he clearly did.

were often obsolete before they were issued. He celebrated his fifty-sixth birthday below ground, his mood dark and his health shattered.

Among those in the bunker with him was Eva Braun. Braun had been his companion and mistress since at least 1933. As the Russians closed in, Hitler urged Braun to leave Berlin. She told him she would not. Her place, she said, was by his side. A witness said Hitler cried, overcome by her devotion. Around midnight on April 28, 1945, he married her.

The next day, Hitler worked as usual. He stopped for lunch around 2:00 p.m. Then he and Eva shook hands with all who were left in the bunker. Together, they went into their private apartment. Both bit cyanide tablets. At the same time, Hitler pushed his 7.65 mm Walther pistol into his mouth and pulled the trigger. After the shot was heard, an aide entered the suite and found both Hitler and Braun dead. Their corpses were carried upstairs to the garden and laid down. Gasoline was poured on them. As Hitler's last followers paid their respects, Russian artillery shells began to rain down. They retreated back to the shelter as the bodies began to burn.

When the fire was out, the wind scattered the ashes. Aides managed to sweep the small amount left into a shell hole. The ashes were covered with earth. Hitler was no more. In his will, Hitler showed no remorse. He spoke again of his hatred for Jews and willed it to his people as his everlasting gift. "I call upon the leaders of the nation and all followers," he said, "to oppose the poisoner of all races, international Jewry."

UNDERSTANDING HITLER

Murdering millions of innocent people was an enormous crime against humanity. It made Hitler

In 2015, ceremonies were held to mark the liberation of the camps, which ended the Holocaust. This Auschwitz concentration camp survivor visited the site at that time.

a unique individual, one whom others have to consider and study. Many books and articles have been written as part of that study. Most are based on a careful examination of the facts. A few, however, distort the truth to put forward a special interpretation. Some writers deny that the Holocaust took place. More than fifty years after the Holocaust occurred, it is still possible to convince naive people that Hitler has been slandered.

We may also be tempted to think that Hitler was so evil that he wasn't human. We may think that, because Hitler's crime was so special, it can't happen again. But of course that is not true. We may also mistakenly think that Hider's evil was obvious. But it wasn't. Many people believed the things that he said about Jews. They had heard them since they were children. Hate is a powerful force, and it takes considerable vigilance and energy to expose it and fight it.

TIMELINE

1889 Adolf Hitler is born in Braunau am Inn, Austria, on April 20.

1903 Hitler's father, Alois, dies in January.

1907 Hitler leaves his small-town home to travel to Vienna, the capital of Austria. There he hopes to study to become an artist. He fails the entrance exam but doesn't tell his family. His mother dies in December.

1913 Hitler leaves Austria for Germany after receiving his inheritance.

1914–1918 World War I. Hitler serves with the German army.

1919 Assigned to spy on subversive groups, Hitler attends a German Workers' Party meeting. He soon joins the group.

1920–1923 Hitler becomes a key Nazi speaker and a party leader. He leads the Beer Hall Putsch, a disorganized attempt to take over the Munich government. Injured, he is arrested and placed on trial.

1924 Released after serving six months of his jail sentence, Hitler completes *Mein Kampf* and rebuilds the Nazi Party.

1929 The worldwide economic depression hits Germany hard. The downturn helps the tiny Nazi Party rise to prominence.

1932 Hitler runs for president. Though he loses, the election cements the party's importance in German politics.

1932 The Nazis do well enough in parliamentary elections to dominate the Reichstag.

1933 Hitler becomes chancellor of Germany.

1935 The Nuremberg Laws are passed, legalizing discrimination against Jews.

1938 On the night of November 9–10, Jews all across Germany are beaten, robbed, and killed.

1939 Germany invades Poland on September 1. Poland falls before the end of the month.

1940 Germany invades France, Belgium, Holland, and Luxembourg. All fall quickly.

1941 Hitler invades the Soviet Union. Special units follow the troops into Russia and begin killing communist leaders and Jews.

1941 Mass exterminations at death camps begin at Chelmno, in German-occupied Poland, in December.

1943 The tide of the war turns with the German defeat at Stalingrad.

1944 Russia threatens Germany's borders. The American and British armies land in France.

1945 The Allies close in on Germany. With Russian troops only a few blocks away, Hitler commits suicide in Berlin.

GLOSSARY

anarchy A total lack of rules or order.

annihilation The total destruction of something.

anti-Semitism The hatred of Jewish people.

communism A society in which private property is forbidden and all property is held in common by the state.

concentration camp A general term for the special prison compounds used by Nazis and overseen by the SS.

death camp A Nazi camp devoted to the immediate mass murder of Jews and others.

Einsatzgruppen Special units that organized mass killings of Jews and others in occupied territories.

euthanasia Ending the life of a person, especially if that person is suffering from a disease.

fascism A form of government in which a dictator has control over the people and opposition is suppressed.

Führer A German word meaning "leader," now most associated with Hitler.

genocide Mass killing, with the aim of wiping out a particular population.

Gestapo Feared secret police unit of the SS with broad powers. The name comes from Geheime Staatspolizei, or state secret police.

ghetto An area of a city set aside for a certain group

of people. During World War II, the Germans established ghettos in occupied countries to help prepare for the elimination of Jews.

humanitarian A person who works to make the lives of others, especially those facing serious hardships, better.

Holocaust Term adopted by historians to describe the mass extermination and murder of the Jews by the Nazis.

manifesto A public, often written, account of a person's or movement's goals or aims.

militarism A heavy reliance on the armed forces to serve a country's problems.

nationalism A belief, especially a strong or unquestioning belief, in the greatness of one's own country.

Nazi General term for Germans and others who followed Hitler. Specifically, Nazis were members of the National Socialist German Workers' Party, or NASDAP.

putsch An armed takeover of the government. Hitler attempted a putsch in Munich in 1923.

Reichstag The German parliament.

subordinate A person who works for a more powerful person.

systematic Done in a careful, organized way.

FOR MORE INFORMATION

Canadian Museum for Human Rights
85 Israel Asper Way
Winnipeg, MB R3C 0L5
Canada
(204) 289-2000
Website: https://humanrights.ca
This national museum was established to honor
human rights in Canada and around the world.
One of its galleries is dedicated to the Holocaust
and also examines the history of anti-Semitism
in Canada.

The Holocaust Educational Foundation
Northwestern University
619 Emerson Street
Evanston, IL 60208
(847) 467-4408
Website: http://hef.northwestern.edu
Survivors and their families founded this organization to promote awareness and study of the
Holocaust. The group focuses on providing
resources, such as research and teaching grants,
for college and university professors teaching
courses that deal with the Holocaust.

Holocaust Teacher Resource Center (TRC)
Dr. Mark Nataupsky, President

Holocaust Education Foundation, Inc.
P.O. Box 6153
Newport News, VA 23606
Website: http://www.holocaust-trc.org
This nonprofit organization aims to provide materials for educators from the elementary school level though the college level. Teachers can download lesson plans, editorials, and other publications.

Montreal Holocaust Memorial Centre
5151, chemin de la Côte-Sainte-Catherine
Montréal, QC H3W 1M6
Canada
(514) 345-2605
Website: http://www.mhmc.ca/en
Founded in 1976, the Montreal Holocaust Memorial Centre educates people of all backgrounds about the Holocaust. It aims to provide visitors with the tools to fight racism and foster understanding between people of different cultural backgrounds.

Museum of Jewish Heritage—A Living Memorial to the Holocaust
Edmond J. Safra Plaza
36 Battery Place
New York, NY 10280
(646) 437-4202
Website: http://www.mjhnyc.org
This museum's core exhibition is focused on the

Jews who lost their lives in the Holocaust. It is organized in three sections, entitled Jewish Life a Century Ago, The War Against the Jews, and Jewish Renewal. The museum also has exhibitions on other aspects of Jewish history in the twentieth and twenty-first centuries.

Simon Wiesenthal Center
1399 South Roxbury Drive
Los Angeles, CA 90035
(310) 553-9036
Website: http://www.wiesenthal.com
This human rights organization is a leader in research on the Holocaust and on anti-Semitism in the past and today. Though it is based in Los Angeles, the group also has offices in New York, Toronto, Miami, Chicago, Paris, Buenos Aires, and Jerusalem.

United States Holocaust Memorial Museum
100 Raoul Wallenberg Place SW
Washington, DC 20024
(202) 488-0400
Website: http://www.ushmm.org
Dedicated in 1993, this museum is on the National Mall, in Washington, DC. Visitors to the museum can learn about the Holocaust, hear survivors' stories, and learn how we can combat anti-Semitism and genocide around the world today. The museum's excellent website has a wealth of historical information.

Yad Vashem
The Holocaust Martyrs' and Heroes' Remembrance
    Authority
POB 3477
Jerusalem 9103401
Israel
Website: http://www.yadvashem.org
Established in 1953, Yad Vashem is Israel's official
    memorial to the Holocaust. It is home to exten-
    sive archives, the Holocaust History Museum,
    the Museum of Holocaust Art, and a synagogue.
    Yad Vashem is committed to the "four pillars
    of remembrance," which are documentation,
    research, education, and commemoration.

WEBSITES

Because of the changing nature of Internet links,
Rosen Publishing has developed an online list of
websites related to the subject of this book. This site
is updated regularly. Please use this link to access
the list:

http://www.rosenlinks.com/HOLO/Hitler

FOR FURTHER READING

Allen, John. *Hitler's Final Solution* (Understanding the Holocaust). San Diego, CA: ReferencePoint Press, 2015.

Altman, Linda Jacobs. *Shattered Youth in Nazi Germany: Primary Sources from the Holocaust* (True Stories of Teens in the Holocaust). Berkeley Heights, NJ: Enslow Publishing, 2010.

Bartoletti, Susan Campbell. *Hitler Youth: Growing Up in Hitler's Shadow*. New York, NY: Scholastic, 2005.

Brezina, Corona. *Nazi Architects of the Holocaust* (A Documentary History of the Holocaust). New York, NY: Rosen Publishing, 2014.

Darman, Peter, ed. *The Holocaust and Life Under Nazi Occupation*. New York, NY: Rosen Publishing, 2012.

Deem, James M. *The Prisoners of Breendonk: Personal Histories from a World War II Concentration Camp*. New York, NY: HMH Books for Young Readers, 2015.

Freeman, Charles. *Why Did the Rise of the Nazis Happen?* (Moments in History). New York, NY: Gareth Stevens Publishing, 2010.

Gerhardt, Uta, and Thomas Karlauf. *The Night of Broken Glass: Eyewitness Accounts of Kristallnacht*. Boston, MA: Polity, 2012.

Giblin, James Cross. *The Life And Death of Adolf Hitler*. St. Louis, MO: Turtleback Books, 2015.

Haugen, David. *The Holocaust* (Perspectives on Modern World History). Independence, KY: Greenhaven Press, 2011.

McMillan, Dan. *How Could This Happen: Explaining the Holocaust*. New York, NY: Basic Books, 2014.

Nagorski, Andrew. *Hitlerland: American Eyewitnesses to the Nazi Rise to Power*. New York, NY: Simon & Schuster, 2012.

Rappaport, Doreen. *Beyond Courage: The Untold Story of Jewish Resistance During the Holocaust*. Somerville, MA: Candlewick Press, 2012.

Rees, Laurence. *Hitler's Charisma: Leading Millions into the Abyss*. New York, NY: Vintage Books, 2014.

Roxburgh, Ellis. *Adolf Hitler vs. Winston Churchill: Foes of World War II* (History's Greatest Rivals). New York, NY: Gareth Stevens Publishing, 2015.

Ryback, Timothy W. *Hitler's Private Library: The Books That Shaped His Life*. New York, NY: Knopf, 2008.

Vander Hook, Sue. *Adolf Hitler: German Dictator* (Essential Lives). Edina, MN: ABDO Publishing Company, 2012.

Weber, Thomas. *Hitler's First War: Adolf Hitler, the Men of the List Regiment, and the First World War*. New York, NY: Oxford University Press, 2010.

Wiesel, Elie. *Night*. Translated by Marion Wiesel. New York, NY: Hill & Wang, 2006.

INDEX

ABOUT THE AUTHOR

Catherine Ellis has been fascinated with history her whole life. She edited *Key Figures of World War II* and has written several books on military vehicles for young people.

Jeremy Roberts has written several biographies for young people, including works on Joan of Arc and Oskar Schindler.

PHOTO CREDITS